Rats Live On No Evil Star
by Allin KHG

2017 KHG InterServ
empallin@yahoo.com
Oklahoma City, OK

in my home town

they kill rats

they line them up

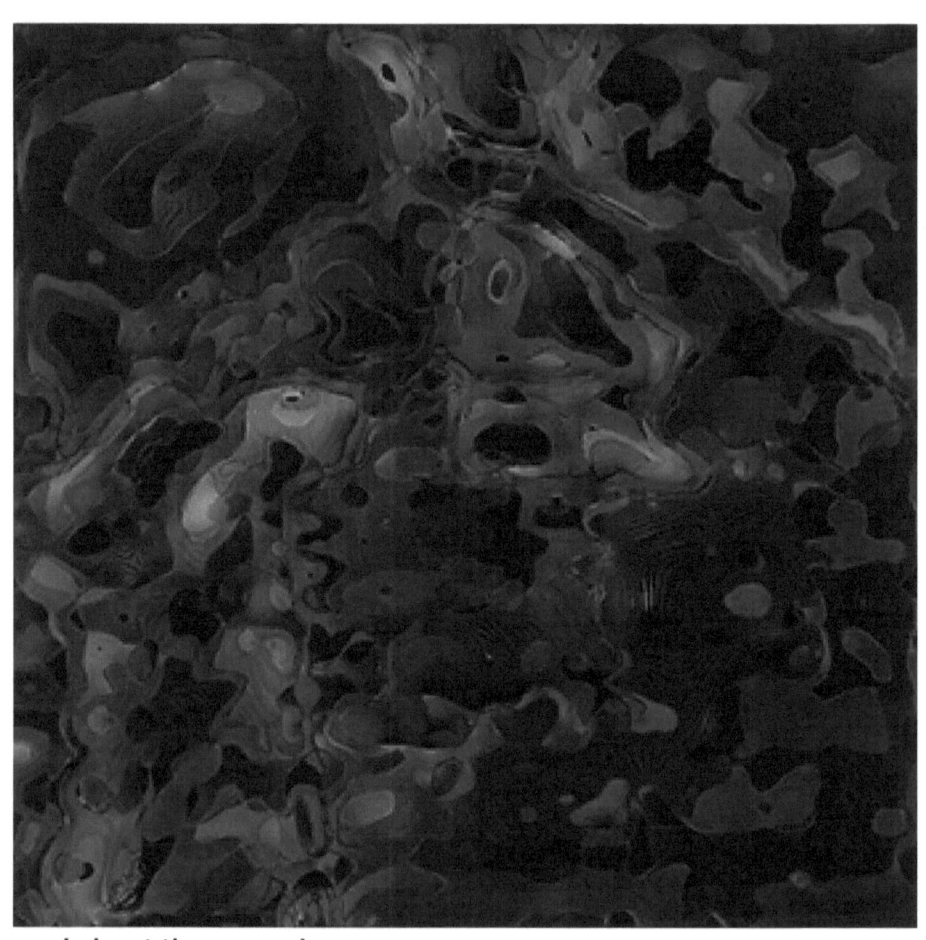

and shoot them one by one

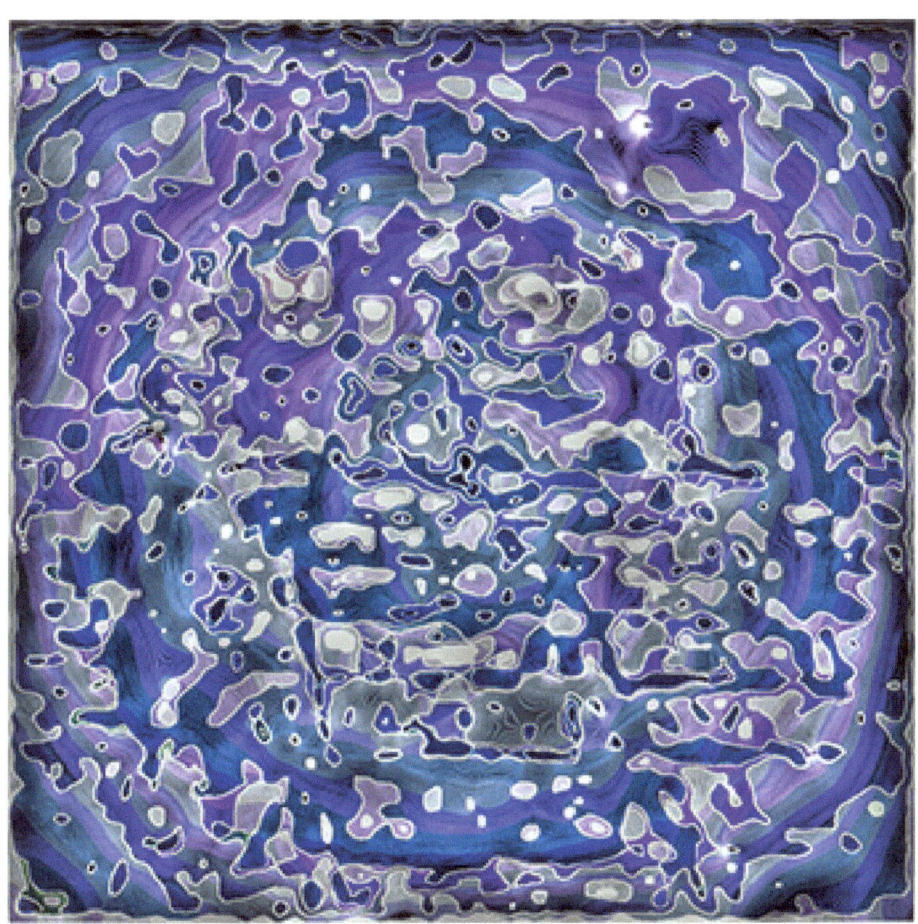

they take them out

as soon as they get a good shot

they run them over in broad daylight

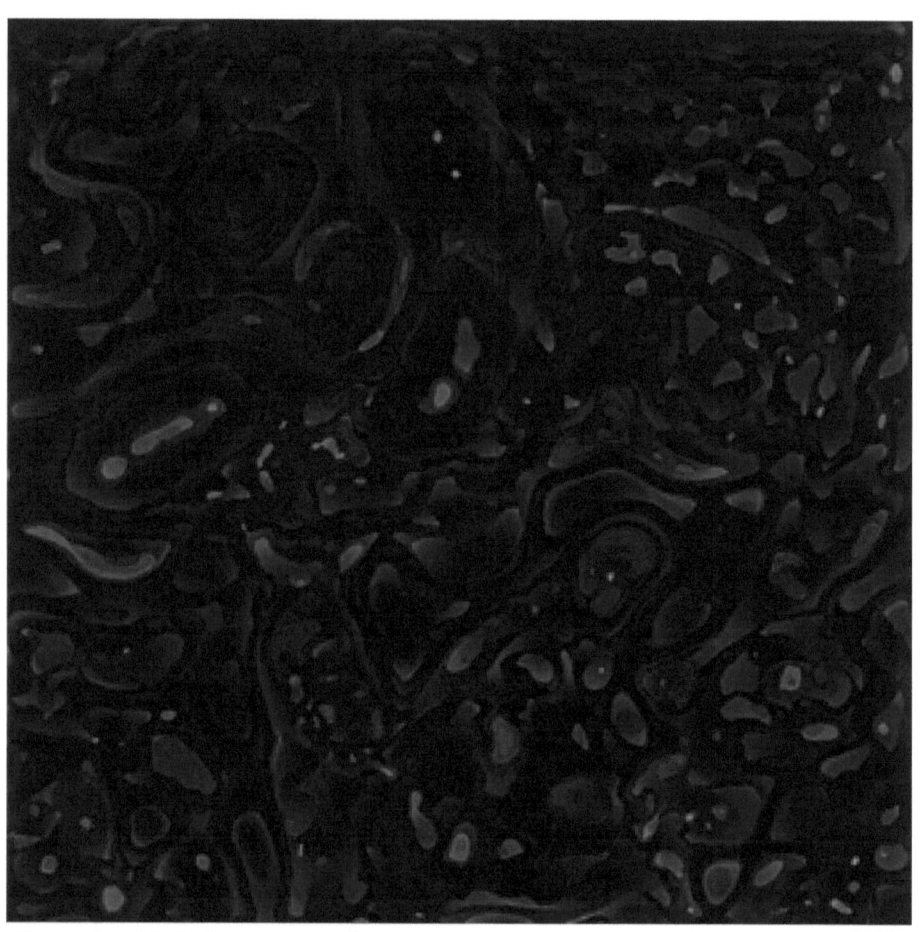
the rats think they are safe

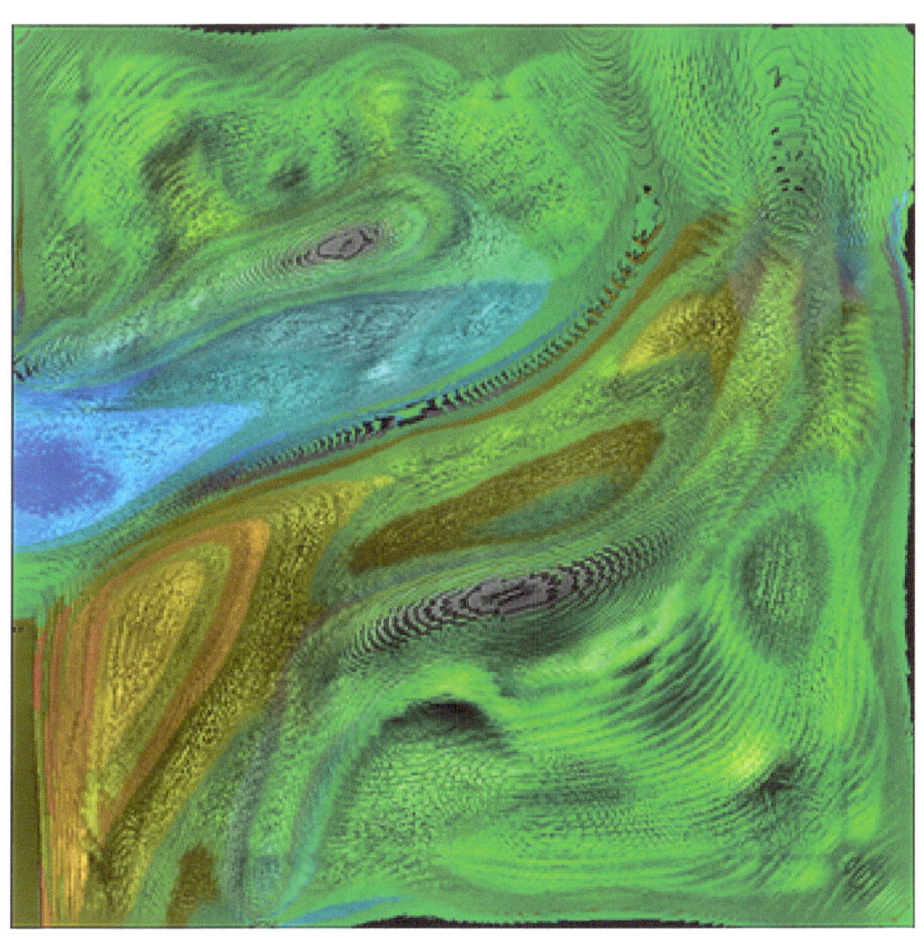

around the monster

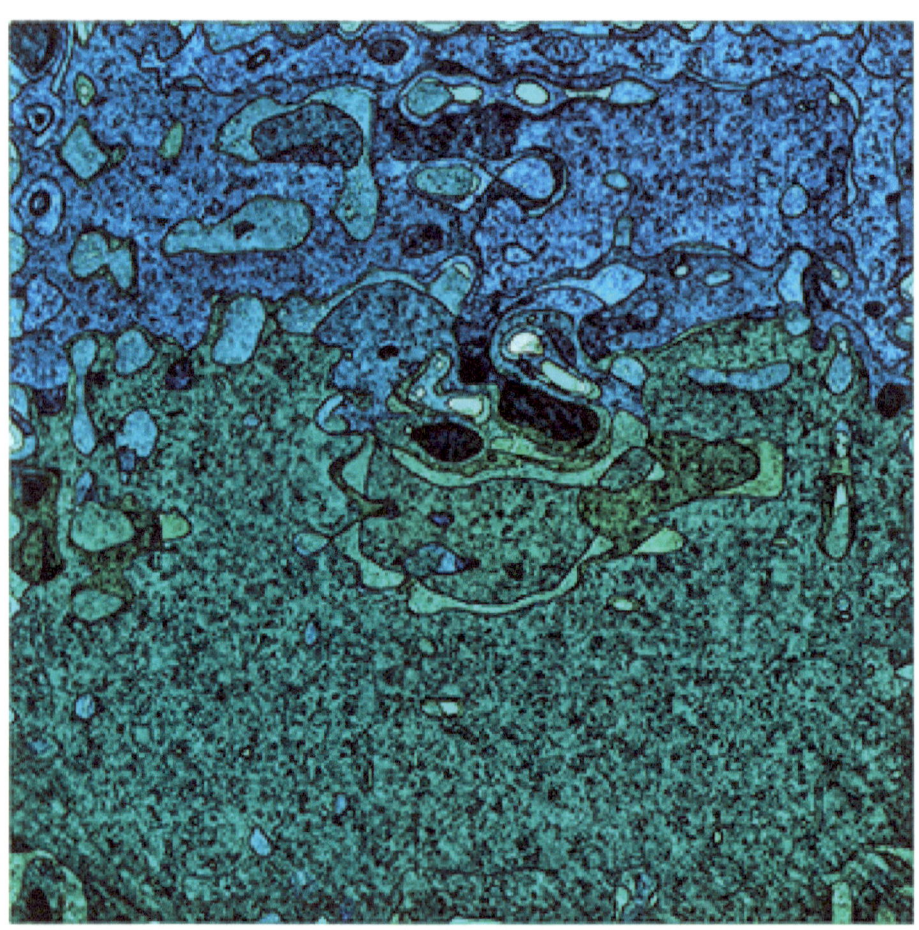

noisy filthy creatures

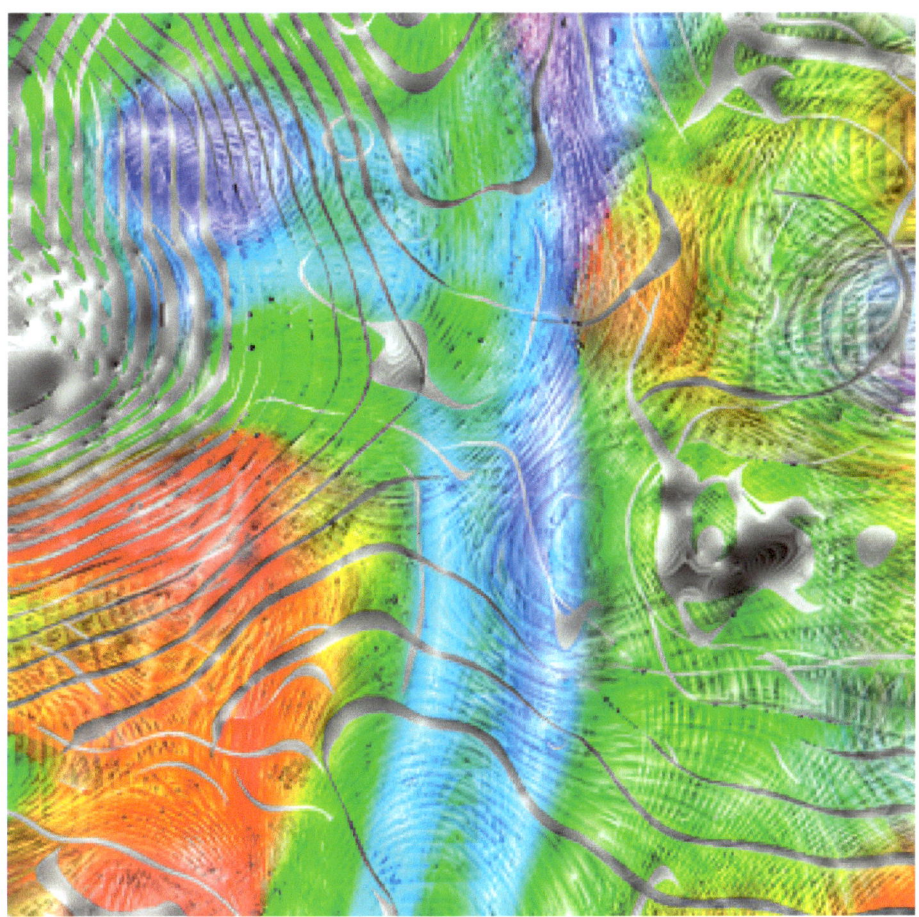

filling the streets and sidewalks

maybe they will be safer in the next town

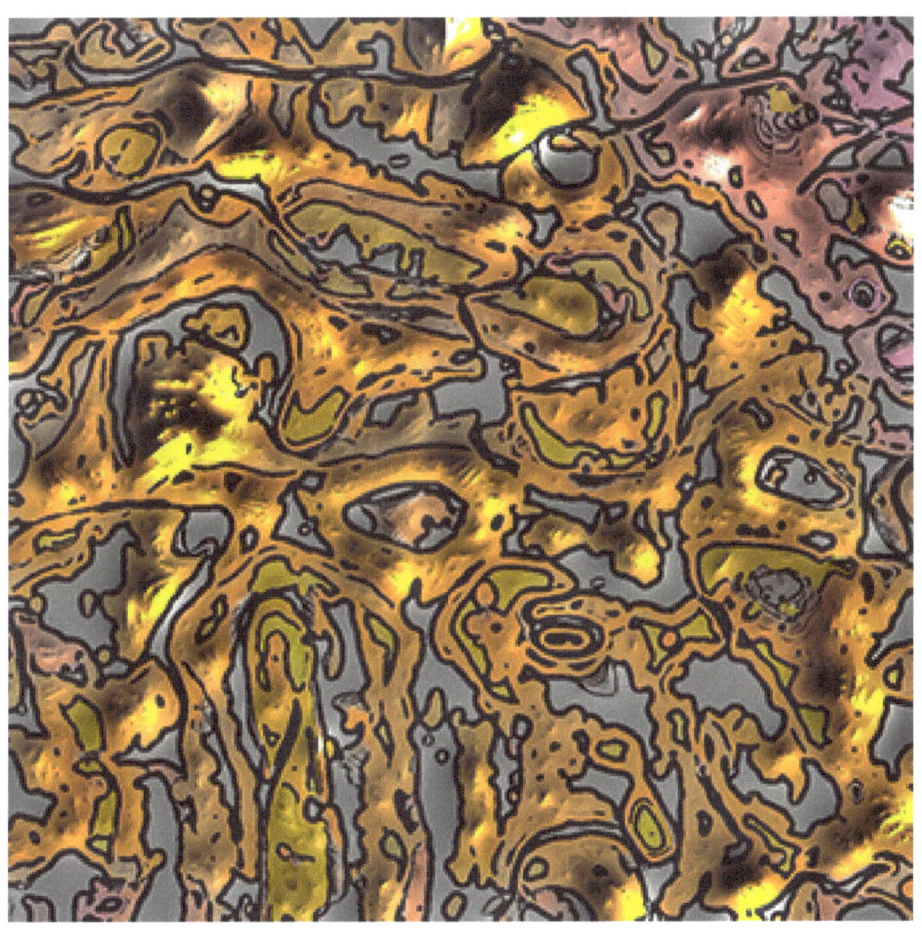

they killed their king with joy

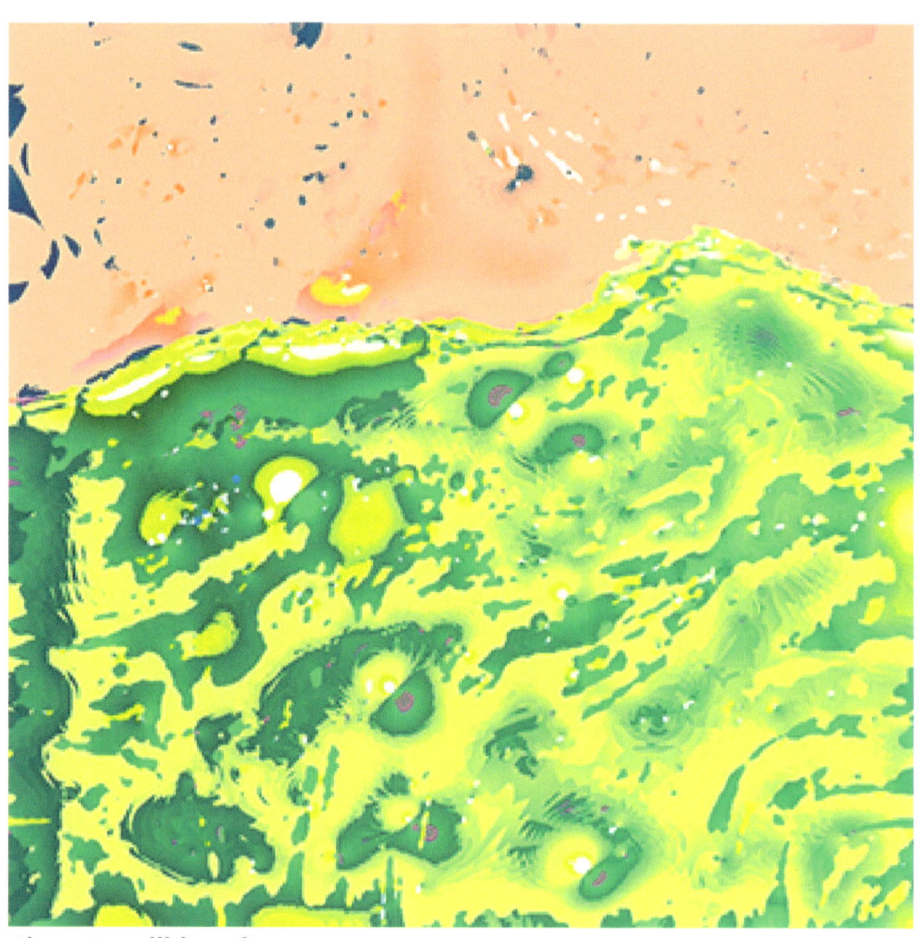

the rats will be of no concern

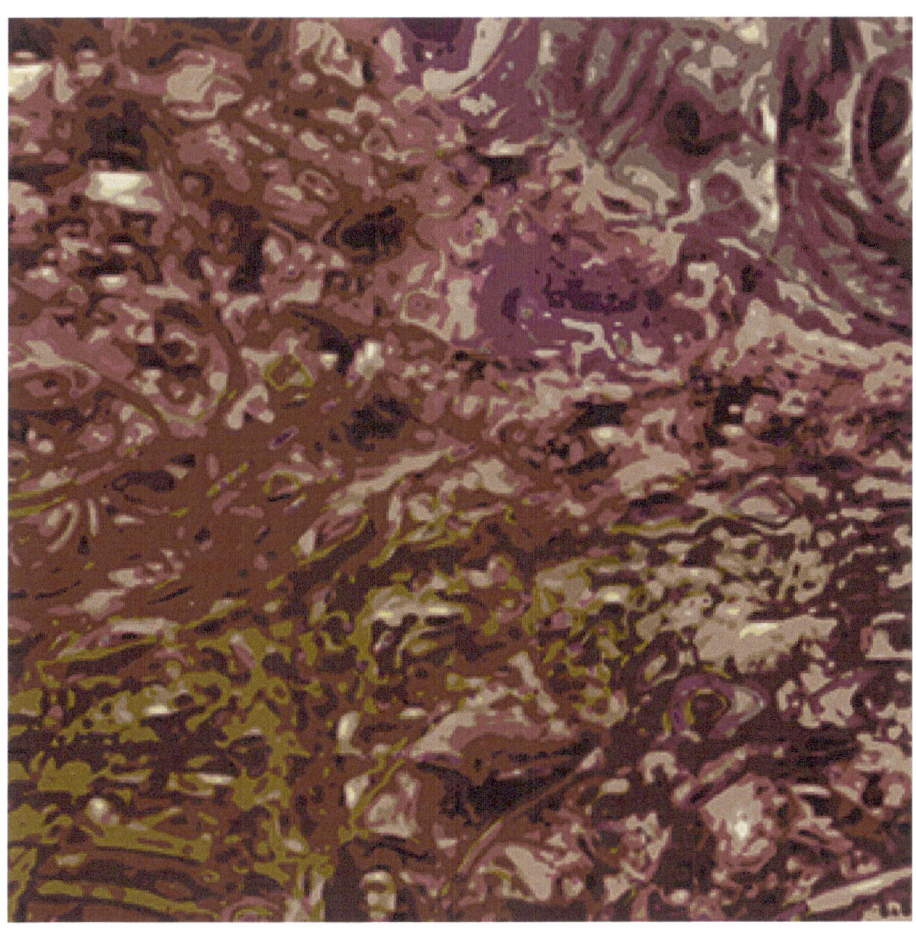

they kill rats as quick as they can

a quick and clean kill

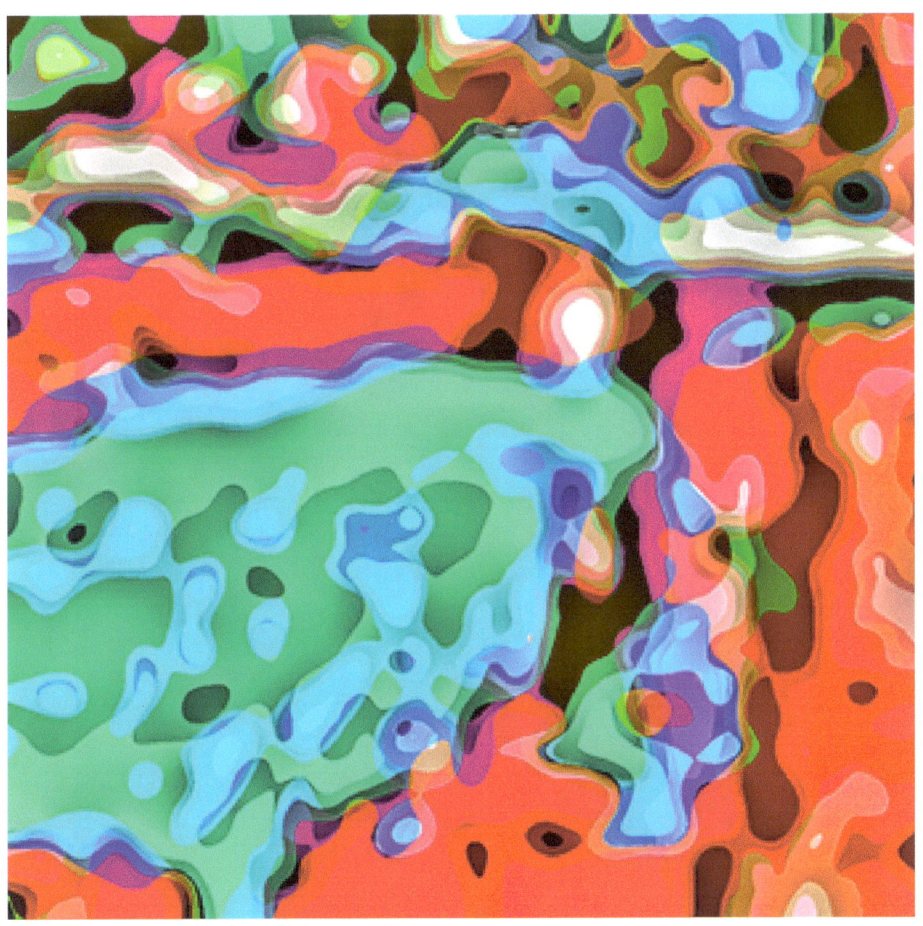

run em over and call it good

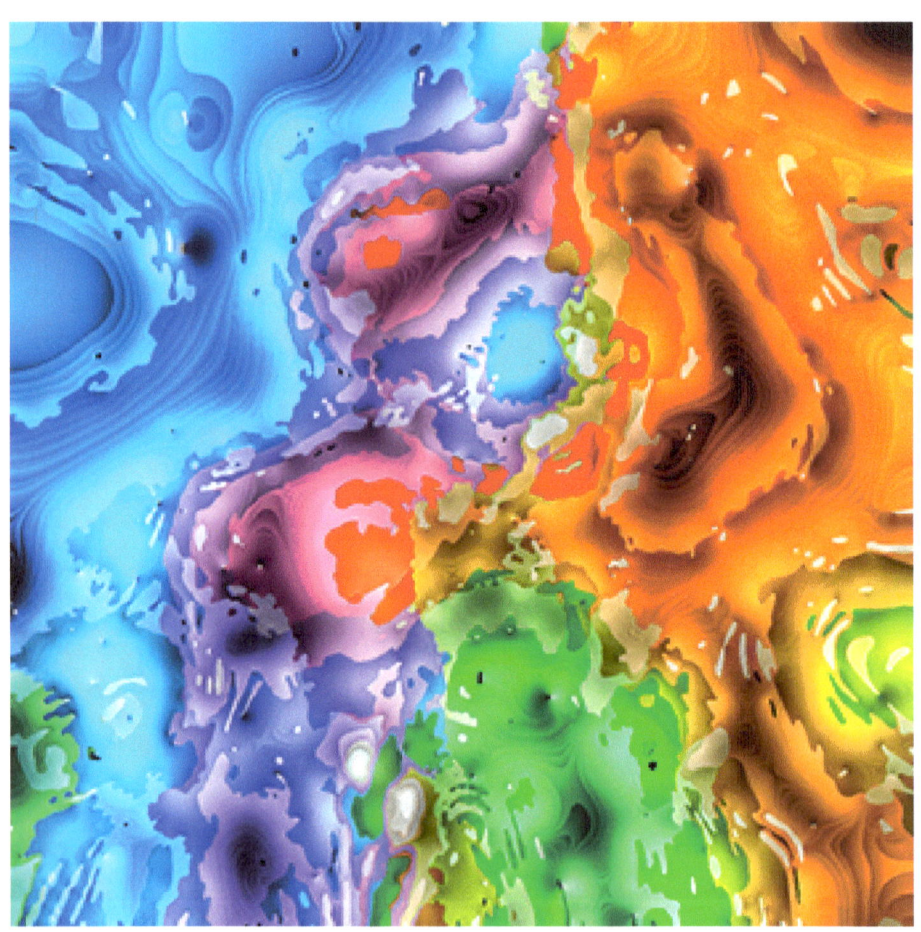

rat eat rat

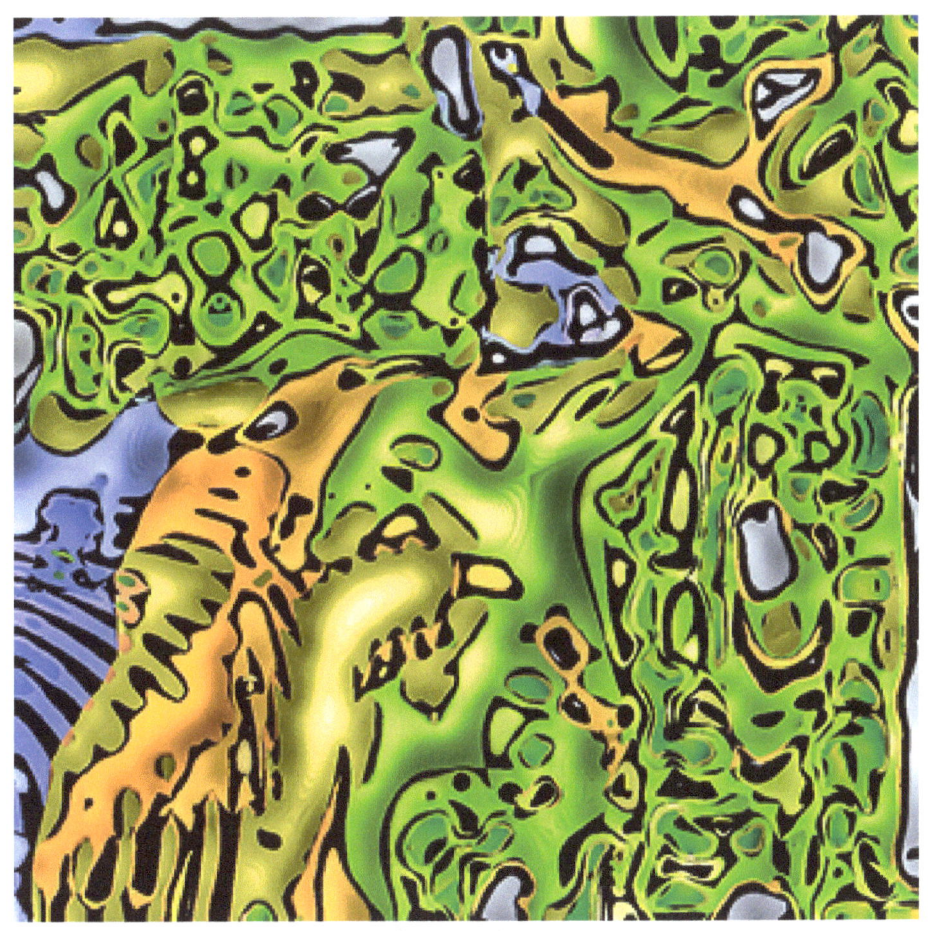

the bigger rats feasting on the weaker ones

a proud display of a lack of respect

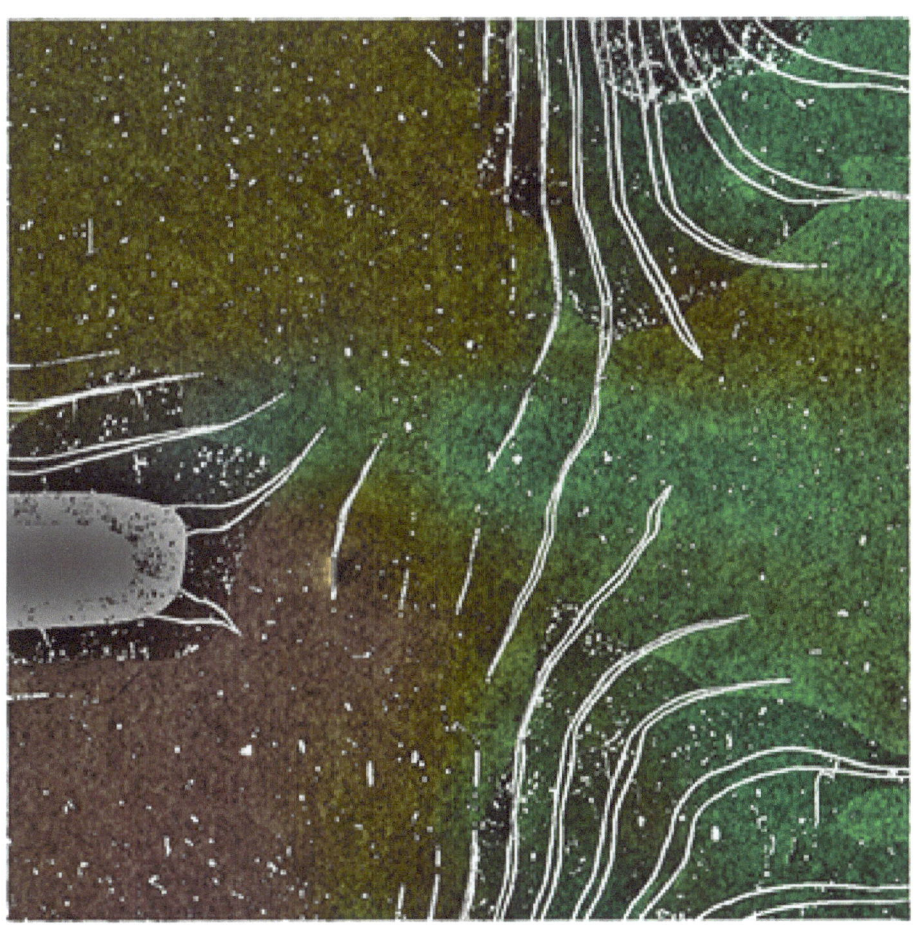

now the star rats

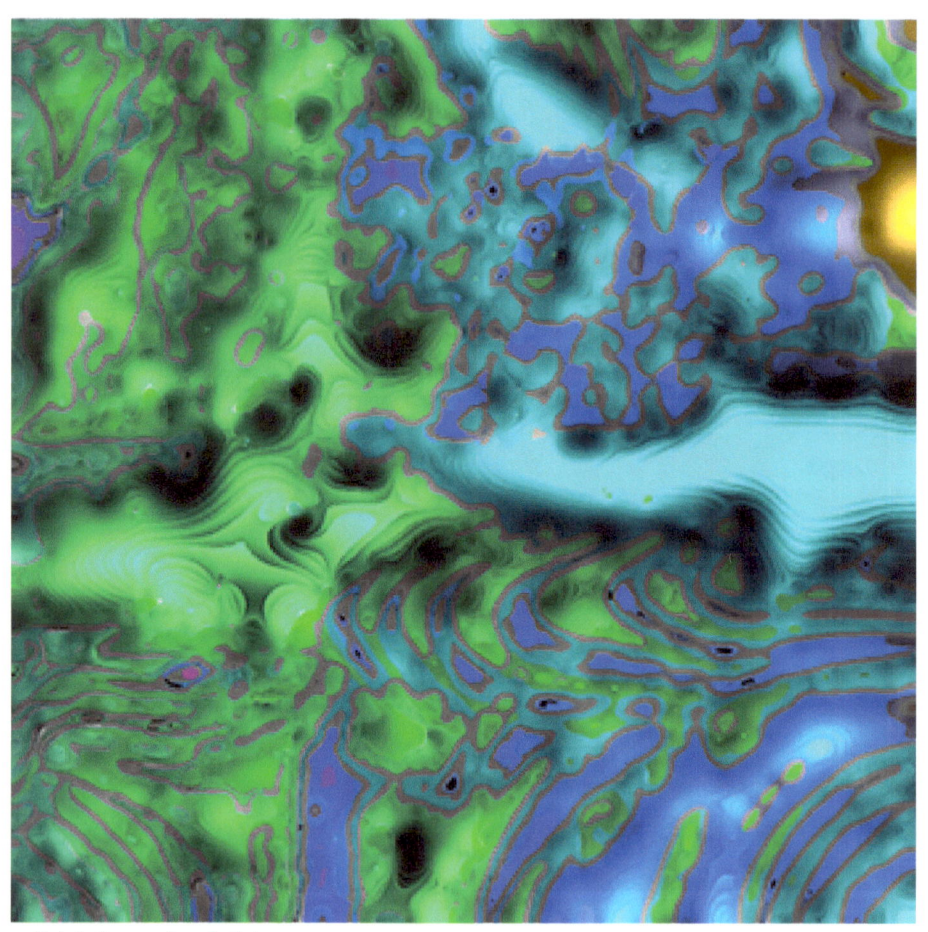

sit high and mighty

on a rotten stinking

www.ingramcontent.com/pod-product-compliance
Lightning Source LLC
Chambersburg PA
CBHW041133200526
45172CB00018B/371